THE SECRETS OF MESCALINE

TRIPPING ON PEYOTE AND OTHER
PSYCHOACTIVE CACTI

ALEX GIBBONS

Copyright © 2020 by Alex Gibbons

All rights reserved.

No part of this book may be reproduced in any form or by any electronic or mechanical means, including information storage and retrieval systems, without written permission from the author, except for the use of brief quotations in a book review.

UPDATES

For a chance to go into the draw to win a FREE book every month like our 'Stoner Themed Coloring Book' (below), and other updates on our latest books, subscribe below!

https://psychedeliccuriosity.activehosted.com/f/1

For daily posts on all things Psychedelic, follow us on Instagram @Psychedelic.curiosity

In consciousness dwells the wondrous, with it man attains the realm beyond the material, and the Peyote tells us, where to find it.

— Antonin Artaud

CONTENTS

A Few Things to Keep In Mind As We Start — ix
What you need to know about Mescaline — xi

1. Mescaline Trip with Friends — 1
2. First Mescaline Trip Leads To Thrilling Visions and Revelations about Life — 10
3. Peruvian Torch Mescaline Trip — 21
4. Bolivian Torch Syrup Mescaline Trip — 29

FAQs — 39
Afterword — 43
Also by Alex Gibbons — 49

A FEW THINGS TO KEEP IN MIND AS WE START

It's important to note that our aim is not to glorify the use of mescaline, other psychedelics, or any other drugs. Mescaline is a mind-altering chemical substance, and it therefore could be potentially harmful to you.

Possessing and distributing mescaline cacti may be against local or national laws where you live. If you are a member of a native tribe that has been using mescaline for spiritual purposes for generations, there may be special laws that protect your religious rights to possess and use mescaline. However, these laws may be limited when it comes to the distribution of mescaline cacti. Make sure that you are aware of any possible legal repercussions before you take any risks.

Also, make sure that you handle mescaline as carefully as possible to lower the risk of overdosing. It's important to understand that different mescaline cacti vary greatly in terms of potency, so ensure that you have a good sense of how much mescaline content is in the cacti that you use. If you are on medication or you have any pre-existing medical condition, avoid the use of mescaline unless you are certain that it's totally safe.

Finally, the stories in this book are meant to inform and to entertain you. They are first-person recollections by people who have been on mescaline trips. We have changed the names of our contributors to protect their identities, but we've left all other details intact. You should also note that these are subjective accounts, so, should you take mescaline in the future, it's likely that your experience might turn out to be different from the following accounts.

WHAT YOU NEED TO KNOW ABOUT MESCALINE

Mescaline is a natural psychedelic compound with the chemical formulae 3, 4, 5-trimethoxyphenethylamine. This hallucinogenic compound is naturally found in several types of cacti, including Peyote, Peruvian Torch cactus, and the San Pedro cactus.

The Bolivian torch cactus also contains significant amounts of mescaline, but it has other psychoactive compounds as well, so it's not advised if you're looking for a pure mescaline trip. Mescaline is also naturally present in certain types of wild legumes, but the concentrations are too low for it to be harnessed for psychedelic use.

Mescaline has been used by natives in the Americas for over 5700 years. Peyote was used by tribes in Mexico, while San Pedro cactus was used by tribes in Peru, Ecuador, and other South American countries.

Today, mescaline is considered a controlled substance. Its consumption and distribution are either banned or monitored in most parts of the world, but several Western countries make exceptions in cases where indigenous peoples use it in its natural form as part of their religious rituals.

In America, Peyote is considered illegal, but it's perfectly legal to possess other mescaline cacti including San Pedro, Peruvian Torch, and Bolivian torch for ornamental purposes. Since these alternative sources of mescaline weren't a popular choice back in the '60s, they escaped the attention of drug watchdogs.

Mescaline isn't as popular as other psychedelics in the street, but you can easily find it if you know where to look. You can get it from dealers in the form of cactus powder capsules. You can find San Pedro and Peruvian cactus in some botany shops. If you live in the Americas, you can identify areas of the wilderness where they grow naturally and go out there in search of them; and also, if you live near a Native American reservation, you might be able to find locals who are willing to sell it to you.

It's difficult to determine which cactus has the highest or lowest mescaline potency. Peyote has about 0.4% concentration of mescaline when fresh and anywhere between 3% and 6% when dried. The San Pedro Cactus varies greatly in concentration; the most common kinds contain low doses of about 0.1% dried, but other varieties can go up to 4.7%. The Peruvian Torch cactus has anywhere between 0.24% and 4.7% mescaline when dried. As you can see, these figures tend to overlap, so it's practically impossible to tell which source will be the most potent, based merely on the type of cactus you are dealing with.

Where you source your cactus matters, when it comes to estimating its potency. For example, wild Peruvian cacti that grow in Europe may have no mescaline at all, while those that grow in South America may contain at least 4% mescaline.

The specific part of the cactus also affects mescaline concentration. For example, many mescaline users have indicated that the outer green photosynthetic layers of the cactus tend to have the highest potency, while the inner white bits have lower concentrations of mescaline.

Peyote dose recommendations: Dosages for a light trip, you need to take 50 to 100 grams of fresh peyote or 10 to 20 grams of dried peyote. For a medium trip, you need to take 100 to 150 grams of fresh peyote or 20 to 30 grams of dried peyote. For a strong trip, you need to take 150 to 200 grams of fresh peyote or 30 to 40 grams of dried peyote. Any dosage higher than these will count as a heroic dose.

San Pedro and Peruvian Torch dose recommendations: As we've mentioned, mescaline concentration varies greatly in these cacti, so it's difficult to make standard dose recommendations. You need 200 to 300 milligrams of mescaline for mild to average trips, 300 to 500 milligrams of mescaline for strong trips, and more than 500 milligrams for heavy trips. The person selling you the cacti might have a sense of its potency, so he might be able to offer you a reasonable estimation of how much of it you might need to consume in order to have the trip you want.

How to prepare and consume mescaline

Mescaline cacti are prepared and ingested using several different methods. They can be sliced into pieces and eaten raw. They can be extracted into a powder and packaged into pills that can be swallowed. They can also be brewed into "mescaline tea."

In many cases, your choice of preparation method will be determined by the shape of the cactus, the dosage you want to take, and the taste profile of the cactus. Most mescaline cacti are very bitter and many users have noted that they tend to induce nausea and vomiting.

To prepare mescaline cactus, you first have to "shave" the plant or peel the skin; cacti tend to have either hairs or small thorns, which need to be removed. You have to be careful when doing this because the green layer just beneath the skin is the part you want and you don't want to waste it.

You then need to slice your cactus into thin layers: If you want to eat the cactus raw, it's easier to ingest it in this form. If you want to dry it, slicing enables it to dry faster and more evenly. If you want to brew it, slicing makes it easier for the mescaline to be extracted during the boiling process.

You can dry the cactus out in the sun, in an oven, or you can use a food dehydrator if you have one.

Those who prefer to eat the cactus raw often combine it with fruits or other foods that help to mask the bitter taste (e.g., orange slices). Most first time users prefer to consume mescaline in liquid form because the bitterness is significantly reduced.

Trip duration

Mescaline effects often start to kick in within forty five to ninety minutes after it is consumed. The trip will then peak at roughly two to four hours from the time of ingestion and, generally, mescaline trips last up to eight hours.

1

MESCALINE TRIP WITH FRIENDS

Liam, Mike, Mason, and I have been experimenting with various psychedelics in the past few months. This time around, we had decided to try out mescaline. We did as much research as we could and we reached out to all our connections until we were able to find a decent batch of dried Peruvian torch cacti.

We received the package earlier in the week, so we elected to try out threshold doses on Tuesday, just to get a sense of what the experience would be like – we all had to go to work, so we didn't want to take high doses on weekdays. We scheduled our main trip for Saturday.

On that first threshold attempt, the dose was so low (about ten grams), and I only experienced a few mild visuals, patterns that synchronized with the rhythm of my breath, barely detectable hand trails, and a minor body buzz.

We decided, based on our trial trip, that ingesting higher doses of the dried cactus would be quite the challenge -- the cactus was so bitter that we could barely handle ingesting the first ten grams. So, we decided to use a pulp extraction technique that we had learned about on the Internet.

We decided to weigh out 200 grams of dried cacti, but I added about forty grams on top of that because I had learned that some of the mescaline could be wasted during the preparation process. We dumped the dried cacti into a pressure cooker, added some tap water (enough to cover the whole batch), and then cooked it for ten minutes. We then squeezed and extracted all the juices from the cacti through a strainer. We then added some more water to the pressure cooker and repeated the cooking process.

The cacti had such a strong smell and it got so overwhelming that we couldn't keep cooking it; we had to let it stay overnight and we had to resume cooking it the next day. The entire kitchen house smelled so terrible that I had to sleep in the basement that night to escape the odor.

After cooking the cacti for the third time and straining it, I tossed out the remnants, even though I was certain there still was some mescaline left in there. I felt that given the amount of dried Peruvian torch we had used, we had collected enough mescaline syrup for a great trip.

By the time we were done extracting the syrup, it was Thursday evening. I checked out the syrup: it was dark, thick, and the smell was as strong as ever. I put it all in jars and placed the jars in the fridge, till Saturday afternoon.

We had planned to have our mescaline trip out in nature through the evening and into the night. We arrived at our agreed-upon site at about half-past three in the afternoon and we set camp. We had invited another friend, Mason, to join us, so there were four of us in total.

We had brought with us a cooler, fully packed with electrolyte-rich sports drinks, hotdogs, apples, cherries, and some other soft drinks. We were totally ready to brave the night outdoors; we had brought a tent and some heavy blankets. Since the site was right next to a lake (on a property owned by Liam's family), we also packed some swim trunks. Liam was in charge of the music, so he had packed a boom box, some CDs, and way more batteries than we would ever need.

After pitching the tent and setting up everything else, I took out the syrup and distributed it equally into four different containers. We learned that Mason was taking Vicodin for an old knee injury and we all agreed that he wasn't in the best condition to trip on mescaline. Still, he was adamant, so we figured that between the four of us, we would be able to look out for him even when we were tripping.

We wanted to wait till sunset to take the mescaline syrup, so we went for a swim to kill some time. At about half-past six, we all started choking down the syrup. As horrible as it tasted, we were determined to force it all down our throats, and we even turned it into a little contest to see who would finish their portion first. Mike won. I came in second. Mason managed to finish his dose after a few gulps, but Liam was too overwhelmed, and he decided to take it slow.

I laid on a blanket, next to Mason, as Mike sat on a bench overlooking the lake. Liam strolled around as he tried to finish his syrup. I stared into the cloudless sky. It had been a clear and beautiful day, and even as the sun was going down, I could still enjoy its warmth.

About twenty-five minutes after downing the syrup, my trip hadn't started yet. My stomach was turning a little and I tried to lie on the ground as still as I could to avoid vomiting. I heard someone spewing though and I looked over. It was Mike. After chugging the syrup faster than everyone else, it became difficult for him to hold it down, so he threw up. A few minutes later, Liam also started to throw up.

Lying there on the ground, I tried to distract myself with my own thoughts. I started to feel the mescaline come-up. It was a strange feeling; my thoughts were more like dreams. I was awake but in a kind of dream state. Ideals in my head weren't just fleeting by; they were lingering around and coming alive. They seemed like facts of life, rather than hypothetical or imaginary scenarios. It was a strange sensation, one that's quite difficult to put in words. Once in a while, I would feel a burst of energy surging through me as my mind wandered from one vivid thought to the next.

About an hour after ingesting the mescaline, I was on a full-blown trip. We gathered around the picnic table and started to share our experiences so far. I mentioned that my stomach was still upset, and I was still nauseated, and Liam said that he felt really relieved after throwing up. I realized then that instead of fighting the urge to vomit, I should embrace it. I figured that the quickest way to induce vomiting would be to sniff the syrup container. I was right.

I felt it coming on, so I rushed to a nearby bush and threw up right next to it. I felt my stomach wrench as I purged out all its contents. Just as Liam had promised, I felt an instant and profound sense of relief; it was like I was reborn. Following my lead, Mason also allowed himself to throw up, but he did it within the camping area, so we had to cover it up with dirt.

We all got back to the picnic table again. The sun was starting to set. I stared at the unvarnished wooden table for a while. The grains on the wood seemed to flow. The closer I stared at the grains, the more they seemed to move about.

I shifted my gaze to a tree right next to the table. Its bark also seemed to flow around, just like the grains of the table. It was like the entire tree trunk was a brownish fluid that was moving around in a clear vessel, leaving behind marble streaks. I thought the tree looked so great, so mystical that I actually got up to hug it. I felt as though the tree really appreciated the hug and I was convinced that it reciprocated it.

After hugging the tree, I shifted my attention to the sunset. Now, I've seen lots of beautiful sunsets in my life; most of them, when sober, and some of them when I was high. This was by far the most beautiful of them all. There were hues of lavender, blue, and purple, blending harmoniously over the sky as the setting sun emitted orange embers off on the horizon.

The sunset looked particularly picture-perfect over the lake. We all went to the dock and sat around the edge with our bare feet hanging over the water, and we just sat there, watching the sun as it slowly disappeared. I felt more blissful and more alive than I had ever felt. Someone remarked that it was like staring at the face of God.

As the sunset turned into twilight, I left the dock and strolled around the meadow next to the lake. My feet were still bare and I felt every single blade of grass caressing my feet as I walked along. It felt really pleasing. My whole body was in a buzz at this moment.

We had gathered some firewood earlier in the afternoon and, as it was getting dark, we decided it was the perfect moment to start a fire. I was tripping really hard by that point, and I started laughing and giggling at pretty much everything. I was like a toddler who found everything amusing. One of my friends would utter a passing remark and I would react as though it was the greatest joke I had ever heard. It really felt like the happiest moment in my life.

When we sat around the fire and started to bask at the warmth, I started to experience amazing open-eye visuals. These visuals weren't overpowering, but they were magnificent. The ground we were sitting on seemed to roll and the trees around appeared as though they were slow dancing. It was fairly dark, but I could swear that whenever I looked at a group of trees that were a few paces away, it seemed like they were waving their branches at me.

The flames seemed to have extraordinarily bright colors. They looked very red at the edges and they were green down below. They, too, were dancing, but to a more upbeat rhythm than the trees.

There was a full moon that night. I'm not sure if it's the effect of the mescaline, but the moon seemed so bright that at certain moments, I totally forgot it was night time. The moon seemed to light up everything, and some tree branches looked like they were dripping with molten gold. I lay on my back and stared at the moon for a while. I could see every single crevice on its surface. It also seemed to start rotating if I stared at it for more than a few seconds, like it was self-conscious, and it was moving just to escape my attention.

After a while, the moon drifted away, and I turned my attention to the stars. The stars were definitely the best part of my entire trip. When I started gazing at them, it seemed like they were all rotating at an axis. Somehow, all the axes were interlinked with barely visible strings, forming all kinds of shapes between them. I could see thin golden lines forming outlines of triangles, squares, and hexagons.

When I moved my head slightly, the shapes formed by the

stars would disintegrate, and the stars themselves would jump around, sending out blasts of red, blue, and green rays, which would spread around the whole sky.

I saw four different stars that were moving in straight lines at high speeds. At first, I thought they were shooting stars, but when I examined them more keenly, I thought there was something odd about them. Somehow in my head, I got the idea that they might be satellites, not real stars. This thought freaked me out a little bit. I started to think that they were put there by someone, maybe the government, or even aliens, specifically to spy on us.

At that point, I closed my eyes, as though that would help me escape the scrutiny of those suspicious-looking shooting stars. For the first time that night, I started to experience closed eye visuals. They were really intense. First, I saw what looked like three faces. It seemed like these people or entities were tribal art pieces that had come to life and materialized on my eyelids. The one in the middle seemed to wink at me incessantly. Like he was trying to hypnotize me.

For a moment, it occurred to me that these or similar visuals might be the inspiration for many of the South American paintings and sculptures that I had seen over the years.

At some point, the three tribesmen started to rotate around. they kept gaining speed, spinning faster and faster, until they all burst simultaneously, and vanished, leaving behind what looked like swirling ribbons of different bright colors.

Whenever I closed my eyes, my buzz would start to get intensely crazy, so I refrained from keeping my eyes shut for long. When I opened my eyes, I noticed that Liam was standing a few paces away, staring in the direction of the moon. I got up and walked towards him, then I stood next to him, trying to figure out what he was looking at.

Looking at the moon this time around, I realized that my sense of distance (or my depth perception) was somehow impaired, and the moon looked like a gigantic ball of warm energy, just hanging over the ground. It seemed to me that if I keep walking towards it, I could literally get to where it was, and I would be able to jump up and touch it. I started to walk in its direction, staring at it the entire time, but I didn't seem to be covering any ground.

After walking for a while, I found myself in the midst of a row of short trees. My attention shifted from the moon and I started to feel as though the trees were slowly engulfing me, like they were starting to produce tendrils with the intention of entrapping me there. I thought about stories I had read in my childhood, about trees, deep within enchanted forests, that could either help or harm people. I started freaking out and I looked back to see where I had left all my friends.

I started to run back to the campsite. In my periphery, there were branches that were reaching out to grab me, and I had to duck at least five different times to get away.

I must have lost my sense of direction while I was running because I came out in an area that looked like a hilltop, or at least a giant ant mound. I stood at the peak for a while and I started to relax again. I could see the entire landscape; there were rolling hills in the distance and they looked majestic under the moonlight.

I finally found my way back to the campsite about thirty minutes later and I found my friends getting ready to retire. I'm not sure if it was an effect of the mescaline, but the tent felt really claustrophobic and uncomfortable, so I decided to take my sleeping bag outside, next to the fire. I felt very tired, but the visuals kept me from falling asleep for several hours. We spent the rest of our waking hours gazing at the stars and telling stories. I fell asleep sometime after one am after my visuals were mostly gone.

2

FIRST MESCALINE TRIP LEADS TO THRILLING VISIONS AND REVELATIONS ABOUT LIFE

My best friend is Native American. I had a lot of fun hanging out with him when we were kids and I learned a lot about his culture. His mother is a highly experienced shaman and is well respected in their community. She would often have other tribe members come over and they would use Peyote cacti for ritualistic religious ceremonies. I often heard that Peyote helped them have visions, which were very important in their traditional religion.

Naturally, my friend and I were curious about trying out the Peyote. We even tried to persuade his mother to let us try it out. His mother was, however, very strict, and she wouldn't let us even go near her potted Peyote plants. She said that my friend didn't yet have mental maturity to partake in the religious rituals, and she said that since I wasn't a member of the tribe, the spiritual significance of the Peyote would be lost on me, and even if I was old enough to try it out, I wound neither appreciate nor enjoy the experience. This made sense when we were still in high school, but when we both turned eighteen things changed.

My mescaline trip started at the tail end of a marijuana

high, so there is a possibility that my experience might have been slightly tainted. Still, I feel that I had a genuine mescaline trip that's worth sharing about.

My friend and I smoked marijuana at his house one afternoon (just a few weeks after leaving high school), and we spent the next few hours enjoying a typical weed buzz. We played video games, lifted weights, and laughed at jokes that wouldn't sound funny to a sober mind. We have a shared passion for martial arts, so we spared a little bit too. We then went out for a walk as the marijuana buzz wore off. We were planning to bring back a bunch of snacks so that we could lock ourselves in his room and finish off the remainder of our weed stash.

However, when we walked back into the house and into his room, we were startled to find his mother standing right in the middle of his room, holding his bong. Apparently, she had walked in looking for something else, and she had found the bong at the foot of the nightstand where my friend had carelessly hidden it.

"Well, are you going to tell me where the stash is? I want to try some!," his mother said. I was shocked and transfixed at the doorway, and I couldn't tell if she was serious. If this had happened at my parents' house, I would have been in a world of trouble. But apparently, in their culture (as my friend explained later), mind-altering substances aren't seen as inherently harmful; instead, they are tools that can be used to experience the divine.

Hearing this odd request from his mother, my friend thought that it would be a great time to negotiate, so he said: "I will let you have some of my weed if you will let us in on some of that peyote tea."

His mum tilted her head and looked up for a second, and

then she said: "well, you guys are both eighteen, so I guess that's fair enough." She then walked out of the room.

I was still trying to make sense of what was happening when my friend's mum left the room, went into her own room, and locked the door behind her. Twenty minutes later, she was still in her room, and I started to think that maybe she was just being sarcastic. However, she soon emerged from her room, carrying two large wooden bowls with colorful decorative patterns.

She asked us to follow her into the living room. We sat down on the carpet. It was twilight and the room was mostly dark. She lit a few candles which shone across the room and cast shadows on the walls, she then lifted one of the bowls up to her mouth and blew over the Peyote tea inside. This caused some sort of hissing sound on the surface of the liquid. She chanted a few phrases in her native tongue; it sounded like some sort of prayer or blessing. She then handed the bowl to her son. She repeated the same thing with the other bowl, which she then handed to me.

We started gulping down the peyote tea. It had a really disgusting taste, but my friend's mum urged us to chug it as fast as we could without thinking too much about it. I had to fight my gag reflex as I forced the liquid down my throat, and soon it was all gone. My friend's mum took the bowls away and she stood up over us.

"You have to be left in solitude so that you can understand the plant," she said. With that, she went back into her bedroom and left us there to deal with the mescaline trip by ourselves. I just sat there next to my friend. Although I had seen many people on mescaline trips before, right there in that living room, I wasn't sure what to expect. I kept waiting for something to happen. My mind was mostly blank, but once in a while, I would experience anticipatory nervousness.

As I waited for the effects to kick in, I must have fallen asleep at some point. I do not remember having any dreams at all; instead, there was absolute darkness all over the place, and my sleep was deep and undisturbed.

I woke up in a cold sweat and it took me a moment to figure out where I was. My friend wasn't sitting next to me anymore. I woke up just in time to see him dashing around the corner as he rushed to the bathroom. In the bathroom, he was grunting very loudly and was swearing profusely. This surprised me because despite his freethinking nature, he was always so mild-mannered and he hardly ever used profane language. At times he seemed to be shouting incoherently, but I could tell from his tone that he was complaining about something.

I looked at the clock and I realized that it was two hours since I had ingested the Peyote tea. I must have been asleep for most of that time, so I must have missed the come up. I suddenly became aware of the fact that I was on a full-blown trip. The candle flames seemed to be dancing rhythmically, and they felt animated. I considered looking around to discover more visuals, but my friend was now cursing in a mournful tone as he violently vomited in the bathroom, and since I couldn't comprehend what he was trying to say, I decided to follow him in there.

As I dashed through the hallway, something bumped into me, and I turned around. I was taken aback by the appearance of the door at the end of the hall. It surged forward in a wild manner, and it started to spin around. It spun right then changed directions and spun left, all in quick progression. It looked as though it was off its hinges and it was bouncing around, just like a spinning top. The freakiest part of all was that it seemed to be charging towards me, like it was angry with me for some reason, and it wanted to run me over.

As the door swung back and forth, appearing to move in my direction, I instinctively went into a martial arts stance. My heart palpitated loudly as I prepared to fight the door. I noticed my clenched fists in front of me; there was something off about them. I could have sworn they weren't mine. They looked like they were transplanted from some kind of giant. They also seemed to be bulging and contracting in a rhythmic tempo, like they were made from some kind of liquid.

I totally forgot about the menacing doors as I focused all my attention on my fists; they were now changing colors and becoming brighter. I opened my fists and my hands turned transparent with blue and green hues.

"What the heck is this?" I shouted, terrified at my own hands. I started to feel overwhelmed, like everything in that hallway (including parts of my own body) were trying to charge at me and harm me. I immediately felt a sense of Deja-vu, like I had been that scared before. The situation reminded me of the most terrifying roller coaster ride I had been on. Just like then, I felt so petrified, and I just wanted it all to end.

Getting to the bathroom was no longer a priority now. I could still hear my friend groaning there. I knew he was just behind the door, but I could swear he sounded like he was millions of miles away from me. It was like his voice traveled through space and time to me. I couldn't be of any help to him because, at that moment, I was battling my own demons.

I decided to head back to the living room; the door had

calmed down somewhat, and it allowed me to pass without any incident this time. I walked to the center of the room and I lay down on the floor, looking upwards.

I noticed that the chandelier on the ceiling was starting to morph into what looked like a giant insect creature. It hovered over me, staring at me with its massive numerous eyes, and extending its spooky legs in my direction. It horrified me and I wanted to look away, but I couldn't. I started to scream.

It seemed like the giant insect was trying to say something to me. It morphed again, this time into a less scary insect that looked bejeweled. It started to fly around very slowly in a circular path. It seemed to emit a weird sound that's just impossible to describe. I feared that if I didn't decipher the message it was passing across, it would get angry at me, and might decide to harm me. I strained to make sense of what it was saying and when I realized that this was futile, I decided to curl myself in the fetal position right there on the floor to reduce the harm in case it attacked.

As I curled on the carpet, I found myself turning around and burying my face into the fiber. Soon, I had forgotten about the giant insect on the ceiling, and I found myself lost in the world of crazy closed-eye visuals. To give you a sense of my experience here, you should know that I have been on high doses of magic mushrooms, salvia, and DMT on separate occasions in the past. None of the closed-eye visuals in those cases came any where close to this one in terms of complexity and sheer awesomeness.

I felt like I was in another world. I was drifting along a blue-lit pathway in space. I was getting sucked into some kind of black hole, except it was blue in color. There was a dark, ominous object ahead of me, and I kept moving towards it. As I got closer, it took the shape of the Orion constellation, and it started to swirl around. I moved so close to it that I thought I was going to collide with it, but then it split into two symmetrical objects, as though they were pulled apart by twin gravitational forces in opposite directions.

As the two objects pulled apart, I was thrown at the speed of light into a beam that emanated from the horizon; it seemed that all the light in my field of vision converged into a cone shape somewhere in the distant and, although I traveled at supernatural speed towards that point of convergence, I could not seem to reach it.

I accelerated further and I started to move in a spinning motion, onwards towards the horizon. I kept spinning and flying at the same time until I found myself in a different world altogether; this one was made purely of light and colors. At the moment, I remember thinking "This is the singularity, I'm in the singularity!" This was the undiscovered realm. The realm that some of the greatest human minds could only dream of; I was there physically, taking it all in overwhelmed by its majesty.

Suddenly, I felt my stomach turn, and there was this urgent sensation in my throat. I opened my eyes, knowing what was about to happen. I remembered that my friend was barricaded in the bathroom, so I ran out the front door onto the lawn. I puked my guts out. All my visuals seized for a moment and I was fully present in the real world. I felt relief almost as soon as I was done throwing up; for a few seconds, everything was quiet and clear.

Then, the visuals started up again, but this time they were milder yet more euphoric. I was still outside on the lawn, squatting a few paces away from where I had just thrown up. I noticed that the grass leaves seemed to rise and form concentric circles around me. They were moving around in those circles. For the first time in my life, I felt like the plants around me were really alive – don't get me wrong, I've always understood that plants were living things as a fact of biology but looking and those animated blades of grass, it seemed like they were bipedal grasshoppers strolling around all over the place.

I looked across the lawn and I noticed bushes with yellow flowers. I had walked past those flowers many times before, but today, they seemed like they were shifting colors as their petals stretched and contracted rhythmically. The petals looked like little snakes crawling from the middle of the flower and retreating back again. At first, it was a little frightening, but then it just became a beautiful sight to behold.

It seemed like all plants in the lawn and the garden, were connected by a series of intricate geometrical patterns. Altogether, they seemed to form a vast, vibrant organism that seemed to have a singular beating heart that infused everything with rhythmic movement.

I stood up and raised my head and I found myself staring at the entire suburban landscape, from the street ahead to the residential houses that sprawled all the way into the horizon, where they seemed to rise into the starry night sky. Everything was outlined with all the colors of the rainbow and decorated with bright lights.

I shifted my gaze to the sky. The stars were bright and they seemed to be drifting towards each other, forming some sort of orb at the center. I thought the orb was a representation of a divine entity, maybe even God himself. The orb then split into geometrically perfect halos that started to stretch away from the center and further off in wave patterns, until they were spread across the entire sky.

Now the entire sky was a vast sea of religious shapes and symbols. Most of them were strange, but I could swear that somewhere in the mix, I spotted some familiar religious symbols, including the Star of David and the cross.

After a while, the symbols in the sky started to stretch out like giant snakes. The snakes descended down and now they were all around me. One of them approached me and it seemed to stare at me, but with non-threatening eyes. It then curled around my body, stayed there for a few seconds, and then uncurled and sped away into the distance in a streak of brilliant yellow color.

I stood outside for a while, enjoying my new perspective of the natural environment. I must have been there for hours, just glued to one spot, mesmerized by the intricate visions, and trying to decipher their significance.

When I finally decided to get back into the house, I found my friend sitting on the couch with his mother next to him. Being an experienced shaman, his mother was trying to guide him through his visions by making him describe them out loud. Most of it sounded like gibberish to me, so I decided to focus on something else.

I looked at the clock again and, this time, I couldn't even make out the numbers on the clock-face. I tried to focus on the specific numbers so I could read the time, but every time the numbers started to appear a bit cohesive, they would immediately dissolve once more into what looked like dark smoke.

The peyote was still in my system and I felt like my body was heavier than usual, yet there was this undefinable sense of freedom that engulfed me from head to toe. It felt as though I was transcending my ordinary self and I was somehow becoming part of my own visions.

I wanted to know what time it was again. Straining to see the clock would have been futile, so I decided to ask, "What time…?"

"It's half past 3," my friend's mother said, "Your revelation is almost over." I calmed down somewhat, feeling this sense of relief. Even though it had been pleasant for the most part, I was eager to make it to the other side of the mescaline trip.

I sat on the couch next to my friend and his mother. Slowly, the visions started to get less and less vivid, until all I could see were slight shifting colors on my friends face. His mother left us alone.

As the peyote wore off, we talked about our visions. I told my friend about the bright colored snakes and the plants outside. I learned that his experience had been very different from mine.

He had seen skeletons, lots and lots of them. At some point, he also started to experience his own body, as that it too was a mere skeleton, with no flesh or organs. He said that his visions were horrifying for the most part. He said that when he was in the bathroom, the whole floor appeared as though it was covered with what looked like big nasty scorpions with glistening stingers.

We stayed up for the remainder of the night and we talked about the meanings of the visions we had. My friend, his mum, and their entire community had always believed that Peyote (and other mescaline cacti) was a gateway into the spiritual world. That night, for the first time, I shared their belief. People had different visions while on Peyote because nature and the spiritual realm had different messages for everyone.

I felt that my key to enlightenment was in having a deeper

appreciation of life: not just my life, but the life in everything around me. In my visions, all things seemed more alive than I ordinarily perceive them to be; the candles, the hallway door, the chandelier, the stars in the night sky, and even the clock, which I always saw as inanimate objects, seemed to come alive, and oftentimes, it looked like they were trying to communicate with me. Even living things like the grass and the flower bushes outside had the ability to move around and to interact harmoniously with each other. The implication was plain to see; there is more life around me than I have been able to appreciate so far.

The Peyote was indeed a gateway; it opened me up to a higher consciousness and, for those few hours, I was able to see life as it really is. Now that my trip is over, I may not be able to see the vibrant life energy in all things anymore, but I know it's there, and I can embrace it and become one with it.

3

PERUVIAN TORCH MESCALINE TRIP

It was six pm on a Saturday evening and I was sitting on my couch, staring at a bowl of dried mescaline cacti. I had placed a carton of juice on the coffee table next to the bowl of thinly sliced and dehydrated Peruvian torch. I had acquired the cacti a few months back (legally I might add), from an online shop, and I had gone through the pain of preparing a batch of dried cacti, and I intended to ingest twenty grams of it for the trip.

Initially, I had planned to distill the cacti in order to extract the pulp, but I decided against it because I learned that Native Americans never use such complicated processes; they just consume raw cacti. I decided that I would have a more authentic trip if I did the same.

I crushed the dried cacti into a powder. I then put a few spoonfuls into a glass, poured some juice over it, stirred it for a bit, and then gulped down the mixture. I repeated the process a few times before I was done, ingesting the whole twenty grams.

The Peruvian torch powder was very bitter, but it wasn't

nearly as bad as I was expecting it to be. I have taken lots of different bitter herbs in the past and I'm used to spicy foods, so I think that might have helped. The texture of the cacti wasn't as slimy as I had expected it to be either – I had learned from online forums that if you rehydrate dried cacti, you need to ingest it before it has absorbed too much liquid to avoid a "snort" texture (which is known to induce vomiting). I had taken this advice to heart. Still, as I ingested it, I made a mental note of the vomit bucket that I had placed right next to the couch. I breathed a sigh of relief when I didn't experience a gag reflex after downing the entire batch.

I had invited a friend over and he came in right after I had taken the cacti. We had agreed that he would watch over me in case I lost control during my trip and did something dangerous. However, he wasn't the kind of guy who would sit back and let someone else have all the fun. He came in with LSD tabs, which he took right away, so we were both tripping at the same time (though on different psychedelics).

The mescaline had a slow come-up. It wasn't a major blast, or drastic inflation to the ego, like the kind I had experienced with other psychedelics. Instead, it was more subtle; it felt as though an invisible burdensome weight was being lifted, and I was increasingly becoming lighter.

I put on some music (a psychedelic mix that I had prepared in advance), and I lay on my back on the couch, trying to relax. I found myself clutching at my abdomen the entire time, trying to fend off the feeling of nausea that was slowly and steadily creeping up.

As I lay on that couch trying to fight the feelings of nausea, I felt very introspective, despite the obvious discomfort (I believe it had something to do with the come up). I started to think about my family, friends, and anyone else who would pop into my mind. I thought about my life and the circumstances of my trip. I thought about what I could gain from the trip and if the decision to take it would be worthwhile.

I started analyzing the people close to me, one by one, as I tried to figure out their motivations: What did they expect of me? Were their intentions pure or self-serving? I also thought about people in my social circle who had made me angry in the past for different reasons. It occurred to me that I wasn't very good when it comes to dispute resolution and that maybe I had unknowingly done some things to set them off. Maybe I needed to relax more and to learn to curb my anger.

At half-past seven, about one and a half hours after taking the Peruvian torch, I started to feel obvious signs that I was tripping. Before that, I would catch a few inconsistencies in the appearance of the things around me, but nothing definitive. To me, the ninety-minute come up was proof that I really had a good batch of mescaline.

The mescaline didn't have much of an effect on the music I was listening to. I have been on other psychedelics before and based on my past experiences, I was expecting that the music would feel either livelier or deeper, but that wasn't the case: it just sounded normal.

Two hours after ingesting the Peruvian torch, my nausea was compounded by a sickening feeling in my stomach, and I decided that it was okay to let myself throw up: I had learned through online forums that the reason you want to fight nausea in the first place, is to buy some time so that the mescaline can be absorbed into the body. However, at some point, you have to give in because throwing up is the only way to get quick relief. Now that my trip was underway, I felt there was no longer a need to fight nausea and pain.

I ignored my vomit bucket and walked over to the sink. I stared down at the washbasin and I noticed that the holes at the bottom were wobbling around. I was ready to let it all out, but after a while, I realized that nothing was happening. After standing over the sink for about twenty minutes, I noticed that my nausea was starting to recede on its own.

Three hours after first ingesting the mescaline, my nausea was totally gone, but I still had a slight discomfort in my stomach. It was at this point that I had a warped thought; I decided that I would force myself to vomit by ingesting another ten grams of cacti. I went into my bedroom, found my stash, weighed another ten grams, crushed it into powder, and ingested it, just as I had done before. However, the nausea didn't come back this time.

After ingesting the additional mescaline and finding out that vomiting was out of the question, I went back to the couch and lay down as I had done before. The visuals were getting intense at this point. All the objects in the room had rainbow-colored auras around the edges. The brighter objects had shifting colors, which seemed to change even when my gaze was completely fixed.

Most surfaces in the room, including the walls and the curtains, were covered with patterns that vibrated and moved around. Some objects that were further away (like a lamp in the corner and a flower vase right next to it) seemed to be pixelated.

After trying for a while to bring the pixelated objects into focus, I noticed that my sense of distance seemed to be distorted. Apart from the few things that were right near me, I couldn't accurately distinguish between what was close and what was further away. For a few moments, it appeared as though my bookshelf was closer to me than my chair, even though I knew that was physically impossible.

At some point, my vision actually split into two. I was staring at the ceiling when I noticed that I had two overhead light bulbs instead of one. I looked around the room and I realized the same thing was happening with everything else. I raised my right arm over my head and waved it around; sure enough, there were two of them, each with red and orange auras around them.

I got up from my couch and decided to get some food. That's when I realized that my concentration was impaired because I couldn't seem to focus on what I was doing. I would set out to do something and, in a few seconds, I would forget what it was because I was distracted by some new visual patterns, or some other thought had crept into my head and pushed that one out. I started talking to myself out loud about what I needed to do next so that I wouldn't forget.

My friend, who was having a trip of his own, came into the room, and he changed the music. He had downloaded some Buddhist chants on his phone, and he decided to play them via my Bluetooth speakers. I found that the chanting was actually helpful in restoring my concentration, and I was able to finish making dinner without much incident.

I sat down for dinner at around half past ten. I didn't have much of an appetite, but I managed to force myself to eat a little. My friend seemed to be hungrier and he cleared his plate in a few minutes.

Over dinner, we got to talking, and I noticed that I was

more attuned to my own emotions and those of others. It seemed like the mescaline had made me more sociable. Usually, when I get into arguments with people, I either get pissed off or dismissive. This time, my interaction with my friend was more positive. I listened closely to him and even when we had different points of view, I could keep my emotions in check, and acknowledge that his opinions were totally valid.

After dinner, I talked to my friend for what seemed like hours. I felt that I was having a normal, naturally flowing, and fruitful conversation. In fact, I felt that I was very articulate and that I had lots of great insights to offer. However, a few days after the trip, my friend informed me that it would have been obvious to anyone looking on that I was tripping. He said that I talked in incomplete sentences the entire time. It was like I would start a thought and lose track of it, so he had a difficult time understanding what I was saying. He also said that I seemed to have a difficult time finding the right words to use, so I would take very long pauses in the middle of the conversation.

My trip peaked sometime around midnight. Even at my peak, I felt I was more grounded in reality than when I was tripping on other kinds of psychedelics. In fact, I was able to make a phone call and even to text a few friends and let them know how my trip was going. I was however careful not to post anything on social media; I still had the sense to be worried about posting something I might regret later.

During the peak, at some point, I noticed that I had two distinct personalities. I felt like I was two separate people inhabiting the same body; this was compounded by the visuals I was having. As I mentioned earlier, I saw things in twos; this effect came back at the pick and it persisted even when I closed my eyes; this led me to believe that I wasn't one entity but two. I thought I had actually gone crazy as I tried to wrap my head around this idea.

It seemed that each of my eyes was having its own set of visuals, distinct from the other. With my eyes closed, I could see geometric towers with green hues on one side, similar patterns with red hues on the other eye.

My sense of time remained intact for the most part, although there were certain minor time dilations here and there. I felt loopy a few times, but I would get over that rather quickly. There were also lots of times that I felt like I had Deja-vu moments; either I was having a thought I was certain I had before, or I saw visuals that reminded me of things I had seen or experienced before.

Suddenly, I found myself laughing hysterically at any random thought that popped into my head. This would mostly happen when I thought of something that I didn't fully understand. For example, I was trying to figure out how to perform a certain Buddhist meditation technique I had read about a few days before, and when I found that I was unable to, it somehow became the funniest thing in the world. I laughed at myself so hard that I had tears running down both my cheeks.

After one am, I got the sense that the mescaline in my system was declining. I started thinking about what I had experienced so far, in contrast with what I had come to expect from the use of other psychedelics. I was already over the peak and I had not gone through any of the classic psychedelic experiences, such as being disembodied or feeling a connection with the universe. Perhaps the dosage I had taken wasn't high enough to set off such experiences.

Still, I felt that I was experiencing sort of a healing effect as a result of the mescaline. In my thoughts, I had resolved to pay more attention to people, and to try to connect with them emotionally, rather than reacting with anger at the slightest provocation. That, I thought, was personal growth, and I credited it to the mescaline.

I was deep in thought for the next few hours. At around four in the morning, I couldn't feel any effects at all; I had returned to my baseline and my mind felt totally clear. I felt very tired, but somehow, I couldn't fall asleep. I had gone to bed a little past four and I just kept turning under the covers and checking the clock every few minutes. Eventually, I decided to start watching episodes of TV shows on my laptop. Daylight came and I was still awake. Fortunately, I didn't have to go to work that next morning. It wasn't until noon that I finally fell asleep.

Looking back at my trip, I find myself agreeing with other users that mescaline is gentler than most other psychedelics. In my experience, it's not the kind of psychedelic that you should take if you want to have an otherworldly experience (perhaps you might be able to get there if you take a high enough dose, or if you take other types of cacti such as Peyote). I, however, think that you should take it if you want to have a carefree and relaxed trip, where you can do some introspection and find out a few things about yourself. You just need a good strategy to fight off your initial nausea and then you are home free.

4
BOLIVIAN TORCH SYRUP MESCALINE TRIP

I extracted mescaline from Bolivian Torch cacti using the Kash Technique. It involves boiling the cacti in water and straining it, over and over, then collecting all the mescaline water and evaporating most of it, until you are left with a thick syrup.

I travel a lot for work, so I didn't have much time off to schedule my mescaline trip. So, I decided to take my prepared mescaline while staying at a hotel during a recent business trip. That day, I made sure that all my work appointments were scheduled during the morning hours so that my afternoon would be clear. I also moved all my appointments for the next day, scheduling them in the afternoon, so I would have time to sleep in the morning after my trip.

I decided to take a dose equivalent to 500 milligrams of mescaline because I was hoping for a strong trip.

By noon, I was done with all my appointments, so I added my 500 milligram dose to a bottle of juice. I got into my rental car. My hotel was roughly thirty minutes away, so I figured that I could start sipping away at the mescaline as I drove. I was under the mistaken impression that it would take up to two hours for the mescaline to kick in, so in my mind, taking the mescaline while driving was just a way to get a head-start on the come-up time.

I was surprised when I started to feel the initial effects of the mescaline just twenty minutes after I started sipping it. I was getting high and I became increasingly worried that the mescaline would impair my judgment as a driver. I slowed down slightly and I tried my best to keep my mind sharp and focused on the road.

The music from the car stereo sounded great. It felt as though the singers were right there next to me, like I was carpooling with them. This helped to calm me down and I started to realize that the mescaline wasn't making me hazy; it was just making the sights and sounds seem more vibrant. My judgment wasn't at all impaired. I figured I could easily drive the rest of the distance without any problem. However, I still decided to stop drinking the remainder of the mescaline until I got back to my hotel room.

While still on the road, I started to experience some visual effects. My visual field was suddenly populated with spots of light afterglow, the kind that you get when you stare at a bright source of light, and then you shift your gaze elsewhere – for a few seconds, you would see an image of that source of light, overlaying whatever it is you are looking at. In my case, I saw afterglows of brake lights, reflections, and other bright things next to the road. Fortunately, these visuals were fleeting, so they didn't have much of an effect on my driving.

I breathed a sigh of relief when I finally arrived at my hotel. Because of my slow driving and the traffic situation, it was almost one pm when I got there. The hotel was hosting several conferences that day, so the lobby was overcrowded. I felt a bit unsettled as I made my way through the crowds of people; I was concerned that someone might figure out that I wasn't sober, and they would judge me for it.

When I got to my room, I drank the rest of my mescaline juice mix as I finished up some paperwork. I was concerned about making errors in my work because of the mescaline, so every few minutes, I would stare at the walls and other surfaces in the room to see if my visuals had gone a notch higher. After a few attempts, I started to notice slight morphing of the patterns on the ceiling and the wood grains on the table and the doors.

I was done with my paperwork by half past two. The body buzz effects were strong but not overwhelming, so I thought it would be okay for me to go for a walk. I didn't like the prices at the hotel room bar, so I figured I could get some snacks and soft drinks at a convenience store nearby. I didn't find a convenience store near the hotel, so I ended up walking around aimlessly, reading the signs over the various stores. Some of the signs seemed to be expanding and contracting in a rhythmic pulse. I was particularly taken by a red "on-sale" window sign that would double in size and then shrink back all while glowing, as thought it was made of neon lights.

I eventually found a store, bought some vitamin water and a few snacks. I noticed a deli across the street from the store and I realized that it was half-past three and I hadn't had lunch yet. I walked over there and ordered a chicken wrap.

As I was placing my order, I noticed that the server was acting really impatient with me. That's when I realized that my speech was a bit slurry. Sure, I was able to communicate without much trouble, but it seemed that I was taking lengthy pauses, which must have annoyed the server.

I found a nice table outside the deli and I sat down to have my lunch. It was at this moment that my visuals started to get really intense. The table was covered with patterns that were moving about rapidly. Everything happening around me – including the people walking down the street, the items on display windows, the outdoor furniture, and even a bike tied to a lamp post – seems to have a common rhythm. It was like the entire world was in sync and I'm the only one who's out of rhythm.

I tried to eat my chicken wrap, but I wasn't able to because of my intense body buzz and the distracting visuals. After only a few bites, I decided to throw out the rest of the wrap and head back to my hotel room. I was worried that if I had stayed out there much longer, I might have completely lost my ability to function normally. In fact, I suspected that maybe I was acting abnormally, and everyone was noticing it, except for me.

I was about a mile and a half away from the hotel at this point and I didn't trust myself to walk all the way back. I decided to get a cab. The first cab I approached was already taken; the driver told me that he was waiting for his fare, a young lady who stopped to pick something up at a shop on that street. He was, however, nice enough to offer me another cabbie's number.

I made the call, but it seemed that I wasn't speaking very coherently because the cab driver asked me to hand him the phone so that he could tell the other driver clearer instructions as to my whereabouts. His fare had come back at this point, so he handed my phone back, told me where to wait for my cab, and as he drove off, he mumbled something that sounded like "get it together man."

I sat on a park bench outside, waiting for my cab to arrive. I leaned back and looked at the sky. It seemed like the clouds above were expanding like they wanted to engulf the entire city skyline with their radiant pillow-white energy. The blue sky seemed to have a very rich color and, for the first time, I understood just how expansive it was. It seemed to extend upwards into infinity.

When I shifted my gaze to the streets and then looked back up into the sky, an orange silhouette image of the street would be burned into the sky, and it would linger for several seconds before slowly disappearing to reveal the rich blue sky again.

My cab took longer than I expected and when it finally showed up, I hopped in, and we drove off. The driver offered a bunch of excuses along the way, but I was barely listening to him. I didn't care that he was late. I kept looking out the window and I noticed that everything that we were passing seemed to leave a streak of diffused colors behind.

I got back to the hotel and this time the lobby wasn't as crowded as before. I rushed back to my room, and I was so thankful to be off the street.

My trip must have peaked at half past four because everything felt so intense at that time. My eyes felt like they were covered with layers of slightly translucent liquid because everything I looked at seemed to be refracted and a little distorted. It was like looking through magnifying glasses that were placed at odd angles so that certain parts of the objects I was seeing seemed normal, while other parts were either bigger or smaller than they were supposed to be.

The intensity of the visuals and the sensation in my body made me panic. I thought that maybe the dose I had taken was too high. I also wasn't sure if my trip would have gotten more intense. I felt that I couldn't take the chance, so I went into the bathroom and tried to induce vomiting.

All I had to do was spit into the toilet bowl a couple of times and there it was. I threw up continuously for about three minutes, and when I was done, I realized that I felt a little lighter, and it hadn't affected my buzz; I was still very high. I also felt quite dehydrated, so I drank some of the vitamin water that I had brought back.

My nervousness and anxiety were building up, so I tried the best I could to center myself. I tried to remind myself that I had been on lots of psychedelic trips before and I had always made it through without any problem, and that this particular trip wouldn't be an exception. I kept drinking water and taking deep breaths until I started to feel a sense of euphoria washing over me. The anxiety was all gone and I started to feel really great.

Sitting on my bed, I started to feel real pleasure all over my body. It was strange, like my whole body – from my skin all the way into my core – was covered with nerve endings, and they were all being tickled at the same time. I sat still and tried to enjoy that feeling for as long as I could.

After a while, I took out my phone to check my messages. The light from the screen seemed brighter than usual, and it created some awesome visual effects. It looked like the letters and images on the screen were changing in-depth, and they were moving around in patterns that were hard to follow. I was still able to make sense of everything on the screen.

I found the WhatsApp icon, touched it, and started

reading messages. I had told my friends about my mescaline trip and several of them had left me messages, inquiring about it. I was able to chat with them pretty comfortably. I was still able to type fast, although my spelling was a bit off. Luckily, the autocorrect feature fixed all issues and all the messages I sent out were very coherent (I checked later).

Chatting with my friends gave me a warm fuzzy feeling. Usually, when I'm sober, I deal with lots of back and forth message exchanges without thinking too much about it. However, when I was on mescaline, it made me feel very happy and loved, like I was a part of something bigger. I felt this sense of oneness with my friends, even though we were hundreds of miles apart.

At five pm, I was done with the WhatsApp messages, so I put on my headphones, lay in bed, and listened to some music. I selected some easy-listen times and they gave me this profound feeling of bliss.

I closed my eyes and I started to see these wonderfully complex multicolored patterns in my head. It seemed that I was constructing these patterns using the power of my own mind; either that or whatever entity was constructing them had the power to convince me that they were my creations.

I could see lots of native tribal images. I thought this was odd because I don't deal with such images in my daily life; I only recall seeing them maybe in books or on the Internet, just a few times in the past. So why would my mind conjure them up? I thought maybe I was peering into a spiritual dimension, one that had been visited by native tribesmen over and over, and perhaps, something was being revealed to me through these close-eyed visual patterns. For several minutes, I tried to make sense of those patterns, but I finally gave up, as other thoughts came to the forefront of my mind.

I noticed that I was able to control my thoughts without much effort. This seemed unusual; after using mushrooms, DMT, and other psychedelics, I had come to expect that my thought would just go wherever they wanted like they had a mind of their own (so to speak), but this wasn't the case with mescaline. I did have a few negative thoughts (bits of paranoia and anxiety), but it was fairly easy for me to reign them in.

After a while, my thoughts and visuals were getting repetitive, so I decided to walk out of my room and tour the public parts of the hotel. I went downstairs and I found that the conference-goers were having a cocktail party in the lobby, and all the way to the outdoor area next to the pool. I just walked around the party as if I belonged; this time around, I didn't have an ounce of worry. I even chatted up a few strangers before I went back up to my room again.

I sat at the small corner desk in my hotel room. As I was placing my hands on the desk, I noticed that they were leaving tracers, so I waved both hands over my face, and they both formed trails. The faster the motion of the hand, the more the trails. When I waved one hand in the direction of the overhead light, I noticed that it had a rainbow-colored hue around it.

My eyes seemed watery and I started to notice rainbow patterns everywhere. Every object in the room had all rainbow colors around its edges. Even when I took out my phone again to add something to my calendar, I kept seeing rainbow ripples around where my finger had touched the screen.

At around seven pm, I decided to take a shower. The sensation on my skin was somewhat heightened. The water felt like it was permeating through my skin and massaging my muscles. It was such a relaxing feeling. The hotel bathroom was equipped with one of those sit-down benches, so I just sat there under the shower head for about thirty minutes, enjoying the soothing feeling of the water. The sound of the rushing water made the experience even more calming and peaceful.

After the shower, I lay in my bed silently for a while and thought about how I had always treated my friends, family, and other people in my life. It occurred to me that I had always taken them for granted, and I vowed that I would start appreciating them more. I made a mental note to buy them small gifts when I went back home from the business trip.

At nine pm, I started to come down a bit, but I realized that my heart was racing. I did some breathing exercises and checked my pulse again; it was still the same. My visuals were getting less intense, and although my experience had been mostly positive, I felt relieved that my trip was starting to end.

I realized that I was very tired; I felt so drained that I couldn't do anything. At some point, I noticed that I was hungry, but it took me an entire ten minutes to decide to get off the bed to get snacks that were in a bag on the desk, just a few feet away.

By midnight, my visuals were all gone and I was trying to fall asleep. Despite the fatigue, I couldn't seem to turn off my mind, so sleep just wouldn't come. I had to call the receptionist to ask if I could check out late the next day; she granted my request.

I fell asleep sometime after four am, and I woke up the next day a few minutes before one pm. I felt groggy and a little hungover, and I could barely keep it together during my afternoon meetings. That day, I didn't eat anything until seven at night. I, however, slept soundly that second night, and I woke up the following day, very refreshed.

I certainly would use mescaline again; the trip was fun and it made me feel great for the most part. I would, however, prefer to take a smaller dose. I would also advise against taking it if you have to work the following day. Perhaps a weekend trip would be better.

FAQS

Why does mescaline get you high?

Mescaline molecules bind with specific serotonin receptors (called 5-HT 2A) in the brain, thus producing the psychoactive effects. It has a working mechanism that is similar to most other psychedelics. Scientists don't yet fully understand why activating those particular serotonin receptors results in psychedelic effects, but many have theorized that during this process, neurons (special brain cells) in the prefrontal cortex area of the brain are agitated and excited.

The prefrontal cortex is responsible for focusing your attention, controlling your impulses, coordination and controlling your behavior, and predicting how your actions will affect you and other things in your environment. So, when the prefrontal cortex is excited, these functions are affected, and you feel "high" as a result.

How long will the mescaline trip last?

Mescaline trips typically last anywhere between eight and

fourteen hours. This duration varies depending on the potency of the cactus and the amount consumed. For instance, peyote typically has a higher concentration of mescaline than Peruvian torch, so a peyote trip may be on the higher end of that range, while a Peruvian torch trip may be on the lower end.

The onset time of the trip is usually between forty five and ninety minutes from the time of ingestion. This is typically followed by a one to two hour come-up period. The peak lasts anywhere between four and six hours and then there is usually a two to three hour offset period as the trip winds up.

The eight to fourteen hour trip is usually followed by a period of aftereffects (where no psychedelic effects are felt, but you still don't feel completely normal). This period typically lasts around six hours, but it may sometimes spillover into the next twenty four hours or so.

What are the side effects and symptoms of Peyote?

Peyote has both physical and mental side effects. Most effects are short term, but there are some that have the potential to be long-term.

The short-term physical side-effects of peyote include: rise in body temperature, heart palpitations, slight staggering or uncoordinated movement, general body weakness, excessive sweating, temporary increase in blood pressure, numbness in some parts of the body, feeling flushed, loss of appetite, insomnia and other sleeping difficulties, as well as severe feelings of nausea, and violent vomiting.

The short-term psychological effects may be desired or undesired, depending on the nature of the peyote trip that you want to take. These mental effects include: vivid hallucinations, feelings of euphoria, a warped sense of time, alterations in one's perceptions, feelings of panic, anxiety or paranoia, alterations in awareness, and a general inability to concentrate.

Prolonged use of Peyote may result in the following long-term effects: hallucinogen persisting perception disorder (this is a very rare condition where regular users of hallucinogens such as mescaline experience disruptive visual hallucinations even when they are completely sober), prolonged psychosis (a condition characterized by scattered thinking, periodic mood shifts, and paranoia; this is also very rare, and it's only likely to occur as a result of prolonged use of high doses of peyote).

What about tolerance and dependence of peyote?

Peyote tolerance develops very fast if it's used repeatedly in a short period of time. If you take it every day, you will start developing tolerance within three to six days. That means that you'd have to start increasing your dosage in order to get high, and you'd be stuck in a vicious cycle. It's therefore advisable to space your trips and leave a gap of at least seven to ten days between consecutive trips.

Peyote also has a cross-tolerance effect with other psychedelics such as LSD and psilocybin mushrooms. So, try to avoid taking back to back psychedelic trips even if you are using a different drug each time.

Peyote is not addictive in the conventional sense. That means it doesn't have the chemical properties required to alter the brain in order to create dependence. However, it can be "psychologically addictive." This means that even if you don't feel compelled to use it, you may still develop a dependence on it because it offers you an escape.

Psychological dependence on Peyote can negatively impact the quality of your life as well as your relationships. If it becomes a problem, you might need to seek treatment (fortunately, users won't have to deal with any nasty withdrawal symptoms).

How long does mescaline stay in your system?

Mescaline is detectable in blood for up to twenty four hours; however, if you're concerned about how long it would take before mescaline is undetectable via a drug test, then that's a different story.

Technically, the length of time within which mescaline can be detected in your system depends on the method of testing that's used to detect it. It also depends on your metabolism and other variables such as your age, your body mass, how physically active you are, how healthy you are, and how well you hydrate. So depending on those factors, it may be hard to pin down the exact time mescaline will completely exit your system.

If you are to take a urine drug test, you should know that mescaline is detectable in urine for two to three days from the point of ingestion. Mescaline is detectable in saliva for up to anywhere between one and ten days (depending on the complexity of the test that is administered). Finally, if you are subjected to a hair follicle drug test, then mescaline is detectible for up to three whole months.

AFTERWORD

After reading a wide range of psychedelic trip reports, it's clear to see that there is a common thread that connects all of them. DMT, LSD (acid), mushroom, mescaline, and other psychoactive drugs open our minds to greater possibilities, and they reveal to us that there's something out there, something otherworldly, something we can't just explain.

Those who are scientifically inclined often argue that psychedelics are just mild toxins that cause hallucinogenic side effects. We have also encountered various reductive views on psychedelics, including the argument that all the documented extradimensional and spiritual experiences are just psychosomatic creations of the users' minds. However, even to the staunchest of scientists, the similarities of these trips is undeniable.

In our research, we have encountered many atheists and scientists who wouldn't pay any mind to the notion that psychedelic use resulted in either spiritual transcendence or mystical insights. These people were adamant and dismissive; they were set in their convictions. However, those of them who were willing to try out one or more psychedelic drugs invariably came out of their trips with a change of heart. A few would admit outright that they were totally wrong, but most would agree that at the very least, there was something there that was beyond human understanding.

The point here is that unless you have had the experience for yourself, you can't possibly get it, and you shouldn't be too willing to dismiss what millions have experienced over thousands of years.

Here are the main reasons why we are convinced that psychedelics do, in fact, reveal the spiritual or the mystical:

Some users experience ego death

There are many documented instances where psychedelic users have experienced ego death after taking high or heroic doses of various substances. Ego death refers to a sensation where you lose your personal identity or sense of self, and you become a bodiless entity who is able to perceive things from a neutral point of view, unencumbered by fears or prejudices.

Ego death can be very insightful and people who experience it find it therapeutic. It's also one of the most spiritual experiences that one can have. Some who have experienced ego death have reported that they were sublimated to the point of being mere souls or spirits, and as a result, they realized that they really were spiritual entities that inhabited human bodies.

Most users feel a sense of interconnectedness

Psychedelics users, even those who take threshold doses, often report feeling a sense of unity or oneness with the universe, with people around them, with nature, or with all living things. That interconnectedness is a core tenet of many religious traditions. For example, Christians believe that we are all children of the same God, and Buddhists believe that we should strive to be one with nature. The interconnectedness users feel, when tripping on psychedelics, affirms both of those beliefs.

Interconnectedness also comes with feelings of love, compassion, unity, humility, respect, and an urge to return to a simpler way of living. All of these sentiments are considered virtues in most religions, so it makes sense that people who experience interconnectedness while tripping tend to interpret it as divine revelation.

The time component is different when on psychedelics

On psychedelic trips, time often seems to move slowly, to move at different rates, to stop, or even to move backward. This is strong evidence to the possibility that there are dimensions other than ours where time is not a limiting factor to existence. On high doses of psychedelics such as DMT, a few minutes during the peak can feel like several days.

Many psychedelic users have theorized that time might be an illusion of relativity; when a trip feels like it's not bound by the linear rules of time, you can be convinced that time itself doesn't even exist. This also reinforces the religious idea that our souls are eternal and we live beyond just these few years that we have in this world.

Many users have experiences that are ineffable

Most psychedelic users experience things that they just can't put into words. Ineffable experiences like these can either be confounding, or they can be spiritually nourishing. We've encountered many psychedelic users who say they just don't have the vocabulary to explain what they saw, but it transformed their lives in ways that are hard to quantify. Sometimes, a person's interpretation of an ineffable experience can be affected by their existing belief systems; some might say that it was an encounter with the divine, while others might see it as an interaction with alien life forms that exist in other dimensions.

Many users experience spiritual visions and revelations

There is a reason why ancient civilizations and native tribes in the Americas have always used psychedelics as part of their religious rituals. Many people who trip on high doses of psychedelics often report experiencing visions of spirits, which come in different forms. Some people hear disembodied voices, others see humanoid entities, and others are taken on journeys through places that don't exist in the real world.

Users experience telepathy or group mind

There are many documented cases where people on psychedelic trips were able to communicate telepathically with spirits or extra-dimensional entities. In other cases where large groups of people participated in mass rituals, there are records of people sharing the same thoughts, energy, and emotions. These are quintessential religious experiences; they are exactly like those recorded in most holy books.

Some users experience some form of catharsis and they feel reborn or re-energized after their trips

Lots of people who trip on psychedelics have reported experiencing catharsis. It involves the release of negative energy (e.g., stress, anxiety, etc.) through an outburst of emotions. Some also experience either simulated or metaphorical rebirths, which are part of many religious traditions.

The bottomline is that if you are not spiritual, or you are not open to the existence of other dimensions or life forms, psychedelic trips will certainly challenge your convictions; or at the very least, you'll be left with lots of unanswered questions, which won't be answered by logic or science.

ALSO BY ALEX GIBBONS

Did you enjoy the book or learn something new? It really helps out small publishers like Alex if you could leave a quick review on Amazon so others in the community can also find the book!

Want to chill and experience the benefits of mindfulness? Want to do something productive while watching random videos on YouTube?

Get this fun stoner themed coloring book to scribble on for your next trip. Search for 'Alex Gibbons Stoner Coloring Book' on Amazon to get yours now!

Thinking about taking other magical drugs? Ever wondered what exactly happens when you take them? Want to make sure you don't have a bad trip?

If you want to read more about the history, origins and effects of Magic Mushrooms, LSD/Acid or DMT, search for 'The Psychedelic Bible' on Amazon!

For daily posts on all things Psychedelic, follow us on Instagram @Psychedelic.curiosity

www.ingramcontent.com/pod-product-compliance
Lightning Source LLC
Chambersburg PA
CBHW070104120526
44588CB00034B/2268